Collection *of* Chaos

Collection *of* Chaos

poems by
Tikuli

foreword by
Kris Saknussemm

LEAKY BOOT PRESS

Collection of Chaos
by Tikuli

First published in 2014 by
Leaky Boot Press
http://www.leakyboot.com

Copyright © 2014 Tikuli
All rights reserved

Foreword copyright © 2014
Kris Saknussemm

No part of this book may be reproduced or transmitted in any form or by any means, electronic, mechanical, photocopying, recording, or otherwise, without prior written permission of the author.

ISBN: 978-1-909849-09-9

Acknowledgements

From chaos emerges new paths. The poems in this book were born from the swirling chaos that was my life a few years ago. Some of them have been individually published and I would like to thank the editors of Mnemosyne Literary Journal, Troubadour 21 and Le Zaporogue for publishing them.

I thank everyone who gave me strength to forge my own path, come what may. I also thank Inditeam and the Indiblogger Network for not only providing the platform to showcase my writing but also for standing by me like a family. Much gratitude must also go to my online poet and writer friends and the readers who encouraged me to write.

Thank you Kris Saknussemm for being a wonderful mentor and friend. You are an essential part of my artistic and personal evolution. James Goddard, you helped me break the mental barriers and find myself. Thank you for being an exceptional teacher and an encouraging friend.

Special thanks to my sons. Growing up with you has been a privilege and I cherish your love, support and friendship. I'm very proud of both of you.

I dedicate this little book to all of you.

A Student Heart

Life in the arts is often filled with disappointment. Such is the nature of creating—or trying to create. Even a great personal success can leave one strangely cool after the initial rush of ego boost dissipates. The one enduring form of pleasure and reassurance I've found actually resides in other artists—to watch an emergent talent begin the complex process of flying on the page. This is the way I feel about Tikuli's poems.

Chaos is the culmination of a profoundly dedicated apprenticeship. In forty years of writing and teaching, I've never encountered anyone more committed to being a writer. Over the last few years, I've had the pleasure of watching Tikuli in real time, practicing her craft and searching for ways to bring forth an inner artistry developed over a lifetime. I feel a personal sense of pride in seeing this work completed and offered up to readers. It's both an ending and a new beginning, and that's always an interesting crossroads in an artistic career.

As with all the poets I most admire, words are living things for Tikuli. But as you will come to discover, they are never deployed for their own sake. She uses them to tell stories. The images, scenes, characters and fragments of visionary empathy that you will find in this book are all rooted in her native India—and yet they reach out far beyond national and cultural boundaries. They do so because they have an interior cohesion of spirit.

Her subjects are often the dispossessed, the lost…the abused. There are undercurrents of sorrow and anger. And yet love shines through, even when it seems to be fading away. Above all, there's a powerful sense of hope at work—a student hearted conviction in the redemptive strength of poetry.

Over time, I've read most of these pieces individually, as they were being written and revised. Now presented with a finished whole, and a whole it is, I take away one message that I recommend to you for continual consideration. Innocence isn't something we begin with and then gradually lose through the hardships of life experience, it's a perspective and a state of mind we may achieve—through perseverance, humility, and an unquenchable curiosity about the world.

I've never met Tikuli face to face, but I feel as though I know her deeply through her writing. That's what real poetry does.

Kris Saknussemm

Collection *of* Chaos

poems dwell in
the possibilities
and
the impossibilities
of the
mind

COLLECTION OF CHAOS

In the rear view mirror
a verse retreats
syllable by syllable
consonant by consonant
as ephemeral as life

The poem
scratchings
from a tumultuous mind

The night
still, reticent

The poet
at the edge of silence

dismantled

The solitude
lingers
like
the smell of rain
slaking the parched earth

Poems
half way home
smudged
shimmering
on the sidewalk

Summer is gone
never to return

poems burst forth
from
walls
fences
facades
boundaries
borders
edges
corners
sidewalks
bridges
buildings
roads
leading to
other roads
streets
that blur into the sunset

changing seasons
city chaos
tired hearts
vacant faces

the smell of sweat
and the stink
of stagnation
From the
incessant dust
from the doors
closed forever
poems burst forth

COLLECTION OF CHAOS

incessant rain
a poetic hybridity
of thoughts

Melancholy stillness,
beneath the street light
a neon moon
a half asleep dog

Brimful of hope
in a plastic cup
an empty bottle
by the wayside

A lone cigarette butt
on the melting tar
slowly turns to ash
burns out

Ironic, she thinks
usually the city
doesn't sleep
but tonight...

She snaps her fingers
no stardust, just a sound
she tries again
then settles for it

She steps into the
pool of light
takes a bow,
the dog trots off

Muddy, hungry,
homeless
destined to be buried
in the graveyard of
anonymity
Traumatized children,
pale women,
grieving old people,
disillusioned youth

Cast away by the nation
devoured
by the fire of hostility,
hatred and greed.
Fleeing
the cracking ceilings,
the crumbling walls
of their homes—
plundered and ravaged.

The giving fields
barren
defaced by war
by bursting shells
and
the splintered remains
of their loved ones
who once had faces
and lives.

Each of them
alone in their loneliness
unsure, unheard, unseen,

drawn by dreams of abundance,
by unfriendly cities,
hostile lands.
desperate for a better fate.
no rights, no identity,
their homeland lost to them

Their past, their personality
their hope taken away
by just one word
Refugees

Little hand-prints
in red on the
door knob
the walls
the furniture
up the stairs
on the terrace floor

I found him sitting
in a corner
his clothes
smeared with paint, dirt,
grass and twigs
his hair ruffled and
sticky with grime

A twinkle in the eyes
his face gleeful
a look of content and pride
smiling I kissed his forehead
and cleaned up the mess.
Years later
again

Handprints in red
dark and dirty
on the burning tar
they had dragged him
through the blood-streaked dirt
his body smeared with the colour
of their animosity

I found him
slumped in a corner

his shirt reddened by the
fire of his heart
that same twinkle in his eyes
a look of contentment—
pride at having saved lives

I kissed his forehead
and smoothened his hair
he smiled with
his bloody and mud caked lips
"Mother, I hope someone will
clean up the mess" he said
as he closed his eyes and slept

She watched the mob with vacant eyes.

Tied for five hours to the tree
blood trickled in a steady flow
down her tear streaked cheeks,
the tattered remains of clothes
hardly covered her broken frame.

The sun stabbed sky resembled
the colour of her blood.

She glanced sadly at her teenage son,
heading the mob
with the husband she had loved

The hysterical crowd was impatient
"Kill the bitch"
"Teach her a lesson"
They yelled.

More shouts, abuse, accusations.
Their contempt burned her
with shame and fear.

Blinding pain shot
Through her head.
A rock hit her forehead.
She winced and shuddered
but drank in the pain,
hurt and sorrow.
Blood from the gash
dripped on the pile of
stones near her feet.

The mob became a blur.

Her heart and body ached.
Her breathing slowed.
Her eyes closed forever,
relieving her of the misery
of being a woman.

The police
like mute spectators
watched the 'mob justice.'
Her supposed crime?—infidelity.
Her silence proving her guilt.
Her punishment—to be stoned till dead.

Near the village square
a shrivelled frame
in tattered rags,
squatting.

Her matted hair
full of small dry leaves
blown by the wind.

Her wrinkled face
bursts into a toothless laugh
echoing the mocking kids.

A dry weed
broken from its roots,
adrift in a sea of abuse.

With her seething heart
and fading memories,
she rejoices in a life well spent.

"Wretched woman they call me!
"What about them?
"Living but still not alive"

The little boy stands alone
On the banks of Ganges,
his head shaved clean
like the sky above.

Moist eyes filled with anticipation
look around at trees and parapets,
three mounds of rice lie on a leaf
Waiting for a crow's touch,
for deliverance of his father's soul.

Above—
a bone coloured sky,
infinite and lifeless, with
scowling patches of cloud
drifting in the midst of silence,
shimmering heat,
burning like a live coal.

Below—
vast expanses
of parched earth,
baked brown.
fields,
dust bowls
ravaged by the merciless sun.

On a scorched tree—
A body hangs.
A child's stricken eyes,
Not really understanding,
keep a watch.
A vulture
awaits his chance.

Sharp as mustard,
His words stung and left
A trail of poison in my veins

The marks that you see on my face
Are the scarred gashes of my heart

Parts of my body hurt
Even from the friction of clothes

I'm used to the metallic taste
Of my own blood

"Perform" he said

His coarse lips
Chafed my skin

Rapacious, savage, monster
With a snake like tongue
His fangs exposed and dripping

Large paws groping, thrusting, tearing
Mauling and ripping my body

Confused, deranged, wet and slimy,
I dragged my pain streaked form
Meticulously concealed

A battered rag doll
With a wound between the legs

Who says "time heals"?
It torments, prolongs

I mulled the wine of memory
Filled glasses, raised toasts
Got drunk

And then one day
Sprawled on the cold floor
I packed my dreams
Gathered my hopes
Threw you in the trash—
A crumpled ball
of ink smudged paper

No longer was I a sacrificial lamb
Or a tasty morsel,
No longer was I a part of your feast

No longer a dancing girl
A marionette
A trophy wife
To flaunt
And
Keep concealed
Behind concrete walls
When not in use

I would rather
Live on the streets
Beneath the open sky
And not be used, abused,
Humiliated

I won't
Be your trophy wife
I won't succumb, I'll fight
My soul is hardened
I am a rock.

A life
gripped in a moment
ecstasy, rapture, release

Bodies consumed
a little death and then
rebirth

Pants, groans, gasps
music to the ears
throb, rise, fall, curtains

Yet another faked orgasm
crushed orchids,
stained sheets

She rolls over
disgust shoots through
the emptiness inside

What a performer!
Dawn to dawn
non-entity

Sex, a compulsion
repulsive yet sacred
a tool to feed
four hungry mouths

An echo

Hunger, poverty,
disillusionment,
a childhood lost.
Betrayal or
a broken heart?

A little mouth to feed,
sold for a few family meals,
an ever growing debt,
or her drunken father's whim,
the reasons are long forgotten

Shame, hesitation,
that awkwardness,
the name long shed
along with the name
she was born with

Her nights aren't free
to dwell in the past
nor are her days,
her life no longer hers,
a swivel door

It is not for her to want, to feel
she wears no fishnet stockings
or thigh hugging skirts
her blouse does not
reveal her ample breasts

She paints her face to hide herself
lines her deep watery eyes—
that can smoke
a man with one look—
with kohl

Every day around the
sinister streets of the city
she practices
the oldest profession
known to mankind

Profession? Or
A survival mechanism?
Her livelihood—
an artist making fantasies real,
an entertainer

You ask, she performs,
the rest is shadows,
the rest is secret
different bodies,
different destinations

No questions asked,
unconditional,
a detached ritual
imitating love
time after time

And yet
in quieter moments
her room grows cold,
there is no escape
from the misery,

The masks fall,
the stagnant stories
of human lust, abuse,
enslavement,
prejudices resurface

A troublesome legacy she caries

A new construction site
all day, up and down,
she carries labours

The soles of her feet
burnt and cracked
bleed the harsh summer sun

In a makeshift cradle
hanging from a nearby tree
her infant sleeps

In that moment when she
wipes sweat from
her forehead

And gives her aching limbs
some respite, she glances
at the gently swinging cradle

The milk in her breasts
oozes through the coarse fabric
that rubs against her nipples

With one arm she balances
the basin of wet concrete
on her head,

She sighs, pulls the sari
over her bosom,
turns to climb the shaky ladder

A naked boy, tears streaming
down his mud caked face
tugs at her sari

She ruffles his unkempt hair
and gives him a sweaty kiss,
he goes back to guard the infant

She has nothing more to give.
Turning back the tide of tears
she works, works and works

There is not time to spare,
to hear her stomach growl
or feel her parched throat

In her vacant eyes
an abstract dream of
four walls and roof

She steps carefully onto
the scaffolding of the building
lust filled eyes follow her

She trades her body
night after night, a double shift
for a single shift's pay

The money snatched away
by the drunk
she calls her husband

Where to from here?
She's fucked if she knows!

She sat huddled in a corner
Staring at the pool of blood
Between her aching skinny legs

Her large eyes vacant and dry
Her trembling body battered
Her soul, bruised and ridden to dust

Her childhood innocence crushed
By someone's scavenging lust
Someone she was taught to trust

He ripped her veil
And shamed her forever
Violating her with a single thrust

Alone, in the shadows of her
Shattered dreams
She tried in vain to wipe forever

The events of the night
Her chilling screams

Her heart, pregnant with
Emotions unknown,
Unheard, unseen

Slowly she closed her swollen eyes
And shut herself to the
Rising shame and fear

Too scared to speak
Too hurt to cry
As the mist began to clear

They found her body at dawn

Along with her clothes
Bloodstained and torn.

Beside her tender fragile frame
A single word was written
in her blood in shame
"Daddy"

Face like a teabag
that's what I remember
about the man

And yes
he was bent double
by the weight of memories
his faraway eyes always
searching for something

Every day he would sit
on the dusty porch of his house
conversing with memories
the cat curled between his feet
an old card on his lap
faded and worn

Nudged by the passing wind
the rickety gate would sway
and creak on rusted hinges

He would lift his head
Eyes catching the sun
His face luminous
With patterns of hope

No one ever came
Nor had they in many years
They said
He passed through life
As a dream

The gate still creaks
With the slightest touch

Poems by Tikuli

The card lies exposed
On the chair
'Happy Father's Day,' it says

I often visit the
abandoned house
off the beaten track

Its yard
no longer tended

Here
In the forgotten places
Littered with broken shards,
Rotting leaves, gnarled branches,
Entwined vines and
Dried unruly weeds
I follow the scent
Of unseen blossoms
I trace my fingers
On the ancient walls
Moist with night dew and
On which
Memory has turned mossy green
In places

I look through the dusty windows
That reflect nothing
The sadness of which
Speaks to me

Then, as the seasons change,
In the midst of decay
The tree of sorrow blooms
Night after night
Romancing the August moon

At dawn
I gather the scent of the night jasmine
And with it
The scent of you
Encased between the white
And the vermilion

Between the known
and the unknown
I float
exiled to bottomless nights
out on dark waters
listless
alone
free

I love the swirl
of words
half truths
promises
and most of all
the lies
so cleverly
stirred
in the cocktail
called love

The obvious doesn't interest me
I prefer the hidden

I want to be part of
the secrets
the wild story-telling
hushed, abandoned
like old stone barns

Listen
to their whispers
look deep
into the hollows
you are in there
as much as
they are in you
hidden in mundane

She stood at the edge
overlooking the valley

Her elegant frame silhouetted
in the moonlight

Her intense eyes,
brimming with grief and pain

Her gaze,
penetrating into the quiet abyss

The maelstrom inside her resounding
in the stillness of the night

Nothing is moving, not even the
dewdrops hanging from the leaves

A small cub rests in peace, curled
between her paws, cold as ice

They had been together for just
night, mother and child

She slumps beside the lifeless form,
licks the furry body

Tucking it closer with her paws,
she embraces it for one last time

The forest watches quiescent

The waiting
the incessant waiting
and the watching
maybe...
just maybe...
the mist gathers around me
thickly...
as if wanting to cocoon me
protect my secret longing
and I
left to my devices and
an illusion of company
raise a toast to solitude

The trees are grieving
there is a strange stillness
a vulnerable stillness and I
enveloped in a deep
heart pounding feeling
listen to the whispers
of the wind and raindrops
the night shivers
with the slightest breeze

Fantasy is reality
reality is fantasy
and in between
there is a poet
on a Ferris wheel

Poems by Tikuli

There is a mystery
unfolding in the steam
from my coffee mug
behind my ears
the temperature rises

I miss the taste of the sun
its sweet heat dripping
from your mouth to mine
I miss the summer
the cayenne dusted mangoes
eaten as they should be
with bare hands and abandon—
in just the way we love

On the banks of the Yamuna
a banyan tree stands tall
its woven canopy of branches
opening up to the sky.

An ancient tree of wisdom
a sage, in a spiritual trance
a sentinel guarding Kali's temple
its exposed roots the locks of Shiva

A tree beyond time
a witness to the city's growth
the awe inspiring ancient guardian
of our historic past

Withstanding the turbulence of life
it holds the cosmos in its canopy,
a centre for life—insects
snakes birds and humans

It gives shelter and shade to
weary travellers, devoted pilgrims,
Tired workers who come
for their midday slumber

Under its cool shade from the
scorching Indian summer
children play on rope swings
hanging from its branches

Women, who come to
bathe and fill pots in the river
gather, laugh, chat and worship
under its serene shade

They tie sacred threads
around the age old trunk—
symbols of love, hope
and longevity

It is a landmark of the city, of a
rich cultural heritage, a bridge
between times past
and times yet to come

Time hasn't changed the banyan tree
since first I saw it, my
small fingers clasping
my father's hand

The only thing that has changed
is time itself

A solitary tree stands
against the dark rain-swept sky,
its twisted branches
reaching out to the heavens,
high above
the mourners lament in unison,
their shinning black coats
glistening

The hearse turns a corner

The sapling you planted
near the pond in the courtyard
has blossomed

The lusty boughs of your mango tree
are laden with pale green; ambrosia
is fragrant on the southern wind

The black bees flock to the nectar filled
mango blossom and fill the
pleasure garden with their songs

From a high branch a cuckoo
calls his mate, his song piercing
the shadows across my heart

Below, the sun flirts with the
water lilies as it warms
the cool waters of the pond

The swing, unused now,
moves gently when caressed by
even the lightest breeze

The days have lengthened
since the blossoming of our love
and summer is lonelier than ever

My hammock sways to music
I cannot hear, as I recall
Those fragrant, leisured days

Our joyful laughter and games,
our feet soothed by the
waters of the lotus pond

Twigs and flowers in our hair from
guilty afternoon naps in the grass,
books left upturned on our bellies

Seasons quickly change,
luscious fruits, long summer
evenings filled with birdsong

The blossoming of our love
in the pleasure garden
our first kiss, lying side by side

And then came the season for grief,
we parted in silence in the early morning
before the sun had dried the dew

Years passed and we were apart, but this year
the lane that leads to our garden
is fragrant with love

The lotus pond is brimming with pink buds
the courtyard is carpeted with golden petals
the air is filled with the cuckoo's call

Won't you come my love

Lemon zest
Daffodils
Ripe bananas
Juicy pears

Grapefruits
Pineapples
Tangerines
Mangoes

Sweet corn and lime
Amorous musk melon
Apricots from
time to time

Sunflowers, Laburnum
Sunbeams in your curls
Mellow papaya
Golden pumpkin

An old swing,
A surprise in the mustard field
Your smile on a yellow afternoon
The yellow brick road

A song 'Yellow Submarine'
A yellow mountain bird
Yellow birch,
maple, beech

Creamy gold moonlight
Over our bodies
Butterscotch in a cup
The sparkle in your eyes

The marmalade skies
Honey dripping
From the corner
Of your mouth

A bumble bee
Dancing among marigolds
Irises draped in sunshine
Primrose blossoms and daylily

A canary singing by the birdbath
Blush lemonade, sweet, with salt
A sunburst margarita
By your favourite window spot

Husked—
Shimmering silks
gently stripped

On a blazing bed of coal
A street vendor
fans the embers

Lingering, smoky aroma
Slow tantalizing turns
Then off the fire

Spiced salt porn
Lime squeeze
Vigorous slather

Mouth anticipating,
First bite
A subtle high

Sweet spicy tang
Melting
Penetrating

Recipe for love
A sensuous
Corny affair

The night spilled darkness
while plunging into dawn
and then
came the rain

Riding on a storm
tapping windows, sighing
Its shrill mournful voice
a requiem for lost love,

Driving its talons heart deep
drawing blood
warm crimson splendour
pulsating with memories

Death raises a toast
as the wet bruised sun watches
from behind the clouds
at dusk

On the far side,
alone on her seat
in the fast moving metro
he spots her

Energy flows between them
she shuffles uneasily
in her seat
glances around casually.

A faded red coat, old denims
try in vain to protect
her slender frame.
The cold bites.

Raven hair struggles to break free
from under her worn out scarf.
in her twenties
she ravishes the viewer

Hazel eyes full of emotion
her cheeks glow red, stolen colour
from her dress or is it from the
biting cold? He wonders.

She flips through her magazine,
keeping to herself,
occasionally pushing her rebellious
curls under her scarf.

Their eyes meet,
she twitches her lips
makes her way to the door
alights at the next stop.

He too alights, from a distance
trails her as she turns
on the empty stretch
half lit by dull street lights.

She quickens her pace
He musters courage and
Shortens the distance
Between them.

Lightning flashes and rain
begins to fall, she shivers
the cold wind
cuts through her slender body.

He notices her walking shoes
making crunching sounds
on the wet pebbled street.
He follows a short way behind.

Pretending to be strong,
without a backward glance,
she walks on.
It starts to drizzle.

She opens her umbrella
filling the bleak evening sky
with white fluorescent stars
beneath the rain

He tries to cover his head
with an old newspaper.
Their eyes meet again—
she looks at him, baffled.

"Cold wet evening, isn't it?
a cup of coffee perhaps?
There's a shop there," he says.
They reach the shop.

"No thanks, I'm in a rush."
She takes another road,
vanishes into the warren of
ghostly houses.

He watches until
only her fragrance remains.
Lavender! He smiles to himself,
as he kicks a pebble along the street.

POEMS BY TIKULI

Canvas of snow
A raven adds colour
Yin and yang

Shadow of the moon
Darkly longing
Rich night sky
Changing patterns
Reminiscent
Of love that was

Yet another citrus night.
Moon,
a sliced lemon garnish
in the tequila sky

My body—
hunger shrouded
in a veil of mist
half concealing

Candles burn
flames flicker
shadows waver
stretch out
shiver

Yet another ritual begins—
but this time
for love

The splintered day ends
now the night will come
dressed in shreds
tugging its blanket of stars
and on its frayed ends
a pale and lonely moon

My innermost desires
Sensuous syllables
In blushed hues

Fiery magenta,
Pinks and whites,
Oranges and yellows
Of Bougainvillea
Draped over ancient walls
And clinging to the bare trees

Secret wish lists
Lingering
Pulsating with hunger
Conjuring up the flesh
In your absence
Watering
Our dreams

I held the sun between my fingers
Reminiscent
—Your face
Crimson with love

Abandoned barn
black tree bones
under a white sky
crows sit watching

Faces
ever varying,
ever concealing
masks

Branches
bare themselves
of rainbow leaves.
Imagination
clothes them.
Colours of winter

Night with all its longings
has come.
A shooting star—
wishes tied to a neon kite—
glides through the dark.

And every moment
before a moment
you are there
so far away
and yet so close
and in your
being and not being
my heart awaits its blossoming

Billet-doux
Like crushed roses
On a white satin sheet
Revealed
The morning after

You sure have a way
with your mouth

Insert the knife
a little deeper
into the soft flesh my love

    Slice the heart
    draw blood

    Your words
    by the way are
    as equally effective

Her warm tear-streaked cheeks
Touched the hard pillow
A sharp pain
Flashed through her
Newly tonsured head
Gone were those long tresses
That swayed with the breeze
And fell on her shoulders
Like a waterfall
Gone with him forever
Her glass bangles lay broken
Glittering shards of memory

A single white muslin
Draped her naked youth
Feelings, affections, desires
Destined now to die
Plunged deeper into
The dark recesses of her heart
Her hopes, her tears, her joys
All within the mournful
Cloistered walls
Of her narrow room
Watched the ghastliness of death
The rite, the pyre, the flames

The chants and wails
Flowed before her in a mist
Like a spell
They strained her lifeless body
Under the dim light of the oil lamp
Lay her humble meal

Untouched
In her slender fingers
A clenched rosary
Prayers for he ebbing life
Her eyes, heavy with sorrow
Began to close

The light of the lamp
Faded into the
Inky Bengal night
Plunging her into obscurity

"Outstanding"
"Cut"
"Pack-up"
the director grins

A dazzling smile
lit up her face
her first film—
a brilliant performance

I looked at my friend
made an effort
to match her excitement
she waved and went to her room

Within minutes she was back
her curls flirting
around her face
like soft clouds

Beautiful
in a bright red gown
she looked ravishing
as a newlywed should

Pain cut through my heart
like lightning
a tear trickled slowly
As we hugged

I clenched the
paper in my fist
a message for her—
"He is no more," it read

Two shadows
Intertwined
Silhouettes
Held captive
By the night aflame

Erotic sculptures
Suspended in fragrance
Sensuous apparitions
Dressed in nothing
But the moonlight

Fiery passion dripping
From their naked forms
Molten bodies tangled
With frenzied patterns
Moving in harmonized ecstacy

I am attracted by your unavailability
the half shut windows where
we sometime connect
between the sound of traffic and the
noise of garbage bins being dragged

Mostly the windows stay shut
but sometimes they jerk open
to test their hinges
a sound, a glimpse, a rustle
and that's it. click, snap, shut

You can create or find
new windows, but for that
you need to know the walls.
Then there is the door to our haven
now blocked by the cherry trees

We once climbed but spring
has long since deserted them.
Trees like love, need nurturing
it takes time and effort
and yes, inclination too

I, in the middle of all this I try
to find solace in your being
and non-being
I have the time and inclination.
For me it's effortless to love

Grim Reaper—
she shadows me
like a jealous lover

Ribbons of darkness
fall over her alluring face
her scythe, a sickle moon
against her nocturnal robe

In the realms of shadows
I hear her sepulchral whispers
she holds me captive
with her hypnotic eyes

She, the harvester of soul
and I the harbinger of light
L'amour fau

You swirled me around
like a moonbeam
draped me around you
on that nameless night.
I still carry the fragrance
of your touch
like the sensuosity of
molten chocolate
oozing from a
moist, warm cupcake.

The muse rises from the ashes
dusted with the silver of the moon.
Sweeps me off my feet.
I ride through the night with him,
the wind beneath my wings.

We make love
Pretend to be lovers

Words sizzle
Glow in our heat
Our fingertips burn
With the touch
A flush rises from the groin
Reaches the head
Explodes

We imagine
We make love
In our heads
Undress
Word by word
Fantasize
Write our own erotic tales

We lay ourselves bare
We love the fluidity ,
The madness of the words
As they melt
On our fervid bodies
Words bind us to the bedposts
In a raw sexual ecstasy

A poem rises
Like the fragrance of
Crushed violets beneath us
Your voice brushes against me—
Like crisp cotton—
Hardens my nipples
Your black eyes come alive

Words swell and thrust
Rise and fall
grasp and crush
And drown in a drizzle
Salt rimmed cocktails
They moisten the lips
My lips quiver, you resist

I sigh, spent
I stare at the screen
A light blinks, dies
In steaming silence
I roll a joint—
Good for the head
The muse rises

Your coat in the closet
a single long hair
oddly familiar

Ring on my finger
no longer valid

Photographs
in old albums
hidden away
purposely—
his photographs
which he doesn't
know I have seen

Maybe he thought
of replacing them
but then could not—
and even if he had
your face would
remain etched in
his memory forever

In his songs I feel
your presence
you sang together
watching sunsets
from the green hills
of our quaint
little town

I catch your fragrance
each time he twirls
a glass of wine sensuously
and raises it to his lips.
You are there in the smile
that starts at his mouth
and twinkles in his eyes

You are there in the mirror
he uses to take a last glance

before leaving the house
and in the first rays
of the morning sun
that caress his body
as he sleeps

Often I wonder—if
the nights we spend together
match the magic of those
he spends with you—if
the fire of his passion
kindles you and sends
sparks of love into the air?

I can see how he made love
to you in his controlling way—
he tries that with me
I feel his passion
his readiness to devour
my ample form—
I feel it reaching a crescendo

And then diminish
as his craving grows—
his need for your passion
for your body
as I lie next to him
consumed in my turn by
his memories of you

Talk more say less
Think more act less
Hear more listen less
Forget more remember less
Empty more fill less
Conceal more reveal less
Take more give less

We leave a lot unsaid, undone
We do everything wrong

We pretend
We deny
And then
We regret
We suffer

We live a heartache

Collection of Chaos

My poems for you—
  drunken boats
  tied to the shore
watching their own shadows

A void
Is not
A void and
It has a shape too
The shape of
You

Dull Vacant sky
Nothing stirs
Not even a leaf
On a drooping
Poplar branch
A crow
Laments
Hope is constant
So is waiting

Just a word from you
Just a word from me

Deepening autumn

The winter
Fast approaching

You break
You change
You expand
And then
There is a release—

Sometimes

You reach the point
of combustion
And then
Nothing—
You wait
It is not yet time

Under the spell of your silence
My words become luminous
Radiate from the centre out
Dervishes
They whirl and whirl
In sacred ritual love

A river of words
Runs through
Where our silences merge
I am haunted by waters

My silence
An abandoned hut
By the bay
Your words
The colours of
Autumnal dusk
The night closing in

My silence
Quietly crawls into the spaces
Between the notes of your silence
Finds refuge
Curls and shapes itself
To the solitude

Feed me words
Serve me clarity
Reason and form
I am tired of enumerating
silences—ambiguous, amorphous

My silence
Winds into a crescent
Spoons your words
In the quiet
Of our shared bed
Unclothed
Unencumbered
Unresisting
Free
At ease
With nothing to lose
Finally Home

My words hang insensible
On the pegs of your silence
Waiting
Until a desire reawakens
Recharging them
To burst forth
With energetic love

Your silence
Wraps around my words
Like ivy growing
On the beauty of ruins
Making the voids visible

POEMS BY TIKULI

My words
Unpretentiously bare
Yours well crafted
Shaped, reflective

Words—
Silent shadows
In the dark—
Imprisoned
A poem
Flips the switch—
Fluorescent

Words
Sepia tinted
Neither black
Nor white
Neither dark
Nor light
Maybe both
Or none
Mercurial

Nothing like mine
So much
Like yours

Mystery
Madness
Chaos
Carnage
Passion
Intrigue
Phantasm—
Landmines
In a poet's mind
Tread softly

POEMS BY TIKULI

Your words
Cayenne dusted mangoes
My silence
A dash of lime—
Ménage a trios

My words
an offering
on the steps
of your silence—
like autumn leaves
on temple stairs
constantly swept
and gathered

POEMS BY TIKULI

Your silence
The hunger
That gnaws
At my bones

My silence-
A prism
Your words
Mirrored perfectly
In lucid prose

My silence
Draped in hunger and rags
Stands at the edge
Of your silence
Opening itself to you

You give
Sometimes in slow measures
At others
In excess
And yet
My bowl remains empty

Your silence
Cold, razor-sharp
My words
A shredded tapestry

You stripped me of my words
Unravelled them quietly
Pulled a good seam I guess
Took the braid of thread
And walked away
There wasn't a single knot
A perfect weave
Of silence and words
But how would you know

My silence stops
At the threshold of your silence
Touches it softly
And for that split second—
Reminiscent—
I live

In those moments of loneliness
When your silence quietly comes
And stands beside me
To watch day become night
I curb the urge
To feel its presence
Lest it feels mine
And moves away

Your words—
Sharp daggers
Piercing soft flesh
Killing instantly

Your silence—
Ice on the tongue
The role it plays—
Freeze and burn

Words
Cookie crumble
Winds of change
Scattered them
Now all I have is
A solitary pain and
A handful of emptiness

Poems by Tikuli

Laid to rest—
Words
Tied in neat bundles
Darkness a ribbon

My words dissolve
As they touch
The edge of your silence
Losing myself in you has
A new meaning now

Poems by Tikuli

Your love—
The scarlet letter
I silently wear

My words
Scrubbed and stripped off
Your silence
Scars remain

Poems by Tikuli

Your words—
Hired assassins

Unlit words
Slumbering
In the shadows
Of your silence
Luminous within

www.ingramcontent.com/pod-product-compliance
Lightning Source LLC
LaVergne TN
LVHW011208080426
835508LV00007B/669